PROACTIVE
Business vs Politics

PROACTIVE

Business vs Politics

William Panachyda, Jr.

AuthorHouse™
1663 Liberty Drive
Bloomington, IN 47403
www.authorhouse.com
Phone: 1 (800) 839-8640

Published by AuthorHouse 05/11/2015

ISBN: 978-1-5049-1093-4 (sc)
ISBN: 978-1-5049-1092-7 (e)

Library of Congress Control Number: 2015907275

Print information available on the last page.

BRIEF
PROACTIVE
BUSINESS VS POLITICS

This small book is a means of defining what the word PROACTIVE could or should mean, as it is not really well defined in any dictionary, and one would think it would be the opposite of REACTIVE, which happens to be fairly well defined, except for one example.

This book outlines how the word PROACTIVE is to some extent being used in the business world, verses how it is being used in the "political" arena, where unfortunately, the only difference between the two words is in the "spelling".

PROACTIVE
BUSINESS VS POLITICS

For the past few years, people, particularly in management positions, have been using the word proactive without really knowing what it means, how or when to use it, and implement its use.

Managers sometimes use the word to criticize others, when they themselves have not laid out the task, the guidelines, the purpose, the procedures to be followed, the services to be provided, so as to satisfy the client(s), thus making the company or the agency for whom your working for better and more competitive than the competition.

In the 1962 Edition of the Webster New World Dictionary, and 1989 printing of Random House, the word PROACTIVE does not exist.

In the 2000 Edition of the Oxford Dictionary, PROACTIVE has the following definition: ("of a person or policy") - "controlling a situation, by making things happen, rather than waiting for things to happen and then reacting to them"

In the 2010 copyright edition of the Oxford American Dictionary, the definition is, "(of a person, policy, or action) creating or controlling a situation by causing something to happen rather than responding to it after it has happened; be proactive in identifying and preventing potential problems)".

One would think that Proactive would be the opposite of Reactive, which according to the Oxford Dictionary has the definition as: "showing a reaction or response: The police presented a reactive rather than a preventive strategy against crime.-compare proactive."

This definition, in my opinion is meaningless, and the example is absurd. The police in the United States of America, as in most countries, do not make the laws, but are responsible for upholding the laws, whether made up by city, state, or federal governments.

As far as I know, if someone is going to commit a crime they don't advertise it; as to who they are, what they are going to do, when they are going to do it, where they are going to do it, why, or how they are going to do it. If they did, than the police could be PROACTIVE and put plans or strategies into place to prevent the crime from happening and getting the bad guys.

So what exactly does this word PROACTIVE mean and how is it to be used, and where and when is it to be used.

As a young mechanical engineer out of college in the 1960's, I started my career in the design, build, construction industry. Many of the design issues revolved around the use of equations to solve the design issues, such as power usage, heat loss/gain to determine equipment size, pipe size, quantities, etc.

The managers of the various engineering departments would review the calculations, and the various designs, and coordination meetings would be held between the various departments to insure that everything is coordinated, that there are no interferences between the various systems, that there are no safety issues, that the construction schedule has taken into account all of the activities of the project, and the potential for Change Orders was zero. After this process of coordination and the final approval from the client is received, the project is put out to bid.

Note: The entire coordination process is not only to check what every department did, but it also develops and generates teamwork within the entire company, and commitment as a team, working together, using the strengths of each player, to ensure the success of the project.

After the bids are received, they are reviewed for Scope, Cost, Schedule, any exclusions, and after meeting with perhaps the three low, most qualified bidders an award is made, and construction begins and is closely watched from ground breaking through completion.

You will note, that throughout the foregoing outline, the word PROACTIVE was not used, because it was non-existent. Should problems arise, as they usually do in any business, there was another equation at the times that was quite simple, that could be used in almost any business, and solve most any problem. That equation was:

S=5(W) H

***S = SOLUTION**

***5 (W) = WHO, WHAT, WHERE, WHEN, WHY**

***H = HOW**

The WHO, WHAT, WHERE, WHEN, WHY, and HOW, had the following meanings, and if used properly, with real facts and documentation, could result in a good solution and outcome, without major delays, and/or costly overruns.

> WHO is responsible for the problem ie, contractor, engineering/architectural

design, material; WHO will pay for cost of fixing the problem?

> WHAT caused the problem, WHAT has to be done to fix it, and WHAT will be the cost both in time and money?

> WHEN can the problem be fixed, and will it affect the overall schedule particularly the "critical path"?

> WHERE did the problem or issue happen, was something missed on the design documents, in the field, or the main office?

> WHY did the problem occur now and WHY was it's potential for happening not discovered sooner?

> HOW can the problem be resolved with as little impact on cost and time?

Should any conflicts arise, due to lack of manpower, material, equipment, errors, etc, then the HOW comes into play on the SOLUTION, be it more equipment, more labor, a redesign, etc and WHO is going to pay for it without impacting the estimate, or the schedule.

The only problem with this equation is that it generates solutions after a problem has surfaced and been identified, and not before. As such, this could cause delays, which could impact the schedule, and quite possibly impact the cost estimate.

Being PROACTIVE could solve this problem early, and be very beneficial to all participants in the project, including the "designers", the owners, and their investors, and the company for whom you are working for.

Long before the word PROACTIVE was generated in the 20th century, a Chinese warrior-philosopher named Sun Tzu compiled what is today called the Art of War, which dealt with the strategy and methodology on how to fight and win battles and wars.

Two books, one by Thomas Cleary, copyright 1988, Shambhala Publications, Inc., and one by James Clavell, copyright 1983, a Delta Book published by Dell Publishing Group, translated Sun Tzu's methodology and tactics for fighting, and winning military conflicts in China over two thousand years ago.

The Preface in Thomas Cleary's book and the Foreword in James Clavell's book, both refer to how the strategies of Sun Tzu on how to win wars, are being used in the 20th century to fight the battles in both business and politics.

According to Sun Tzu, wining wars is not just the use of overwhelming manpower, but rather through; Planning, Resources, Organization, Adapting, Conditions, Time, Intelligence, Verifying, Evaluation.

Several years later I got the opportunity to read, PATTON ON LEADERSHIP, Strategic Lessons For Corporate Warfare, copyright 1999 Prentice Hall Press, by Alan Axelrod, Foreword by William A. Cohen, Major General, USAF, Ret., and Preface by George Steinbrenner Ill, owner of the New York Yankees.

The book outlined the leadership skills, tactics, planning, and determination that General Patton used in World War II, to defeat the enemy, at any time, any place, under any circumstances, and how the tactics and principals of Gen. Patton could be and were used, by Mr. Steinbrenner in operating the best major league baseball team in the history of the sport business.

While none of these three books use the word PROACTIVE, the theme and ideas of all three books, revolved around a number of the same parameters.

Evaluating everything connected with the plan of attack and the progress of the task at hand, whether it be a battle or a business endeavour, includes evaluating personnel, resources, time, cost (in war its lives, in business its money), constantly, so that when problems arise, and they will, the changes that have to be made, are made in an orderly and timely fashion, so as not to create confusion, which could cause delays, higher costs, and disparity within the team, thereby diluting the success of the project.

After reading these books, the message is, that to succeed in the business world one must understand the risks, and to be committed to the task, and through Planning, Responsibility, Organization, Accountability, Communications, Teamwork, Identifying potential problems early, Validating everything, and Excelling on what you set out to do and accomplish; in a word be:

PROACTIVE

If most, if not all endeavours, business or otherwise, used the concept of being PROACTIVE effectively, they could be very successful.

In 1993 when I was working for a major construction management company in New York City, I was asked by the President if I would consider going to Brasil as Chief

Operating Officer, for a joint venture between the company I was working for and a Brasilian real estate developer.

As I didn't know about this relationship, I thought this was some kind of a joke, however, he was serious, and after visiting Brasil with the President, and meeting with the head of the Brasilian real estate company, I accepted the position, which was to be for a period of 2 years, which turned into 10.

One thing I wanted to do was to have the entire staff, Brasilian and the few Americans, that l asked to join me, was to work toward the same goals, and to be successful in what we as a "team" were working for, and to be better than the competition.

I prepared some seminars in 1994, the subject of which was: Acting In Anticipation of Future

Problems, see insert, which was based on being PROACTIVE. As there was no definition of the word proactive at the time, 1 used the word "reactive" for generating a definition for the word "proactive".

The result was teamwork, and we trusted each other, and were quite successful, as a joint venture, and as a team, that would get projects done on time and on or below the original estimate.

In 1995, a problem was discovered regarding the misuse of joint venture funds by the Brasilian company. We, the American company, broke away, and I was asked to stay on as General Manager, and continue operations in Brasil, as the only fully operational branch outside the United States.

To do this, I needed many of the Brasilian staff, which the Brasilian company did not want to permit, to which I asked why, and don't they have a right to make their own choice and decisions.

The result was that I asked 50 people to join, 49 did, and we continued for another eight years, until the American company was bought by a German company, which was in the same business, and unfortunately, for me and my staff, the only place in the whole world where we competed was in Brasil, and I was told to shut down operations, and turn everything over to the other "company", which became a major problem, but being proactive solved most of the issues that arose as a result of this turnover.

So what does PROACTIVE mean for business and how is it to be used? By assigning a meaning for each of the letters in the word, one could get the following:

P - be PLANNING ahead, and seeing to it that all those connected with the project are familiar with the PLAN to finish early, and ask who, what, where, when, and why there may be potential problems.

R - be RESPONSIBLE, for your actions, and those of your team, which should include everyone connected with and assigned to the various projects, and that the REPORTS reflect the status of everything, including potential problems, and possible solutions.

O - be ORGANIZED and OPEN book, for in doing so, potential problems and solutions can be identified early, saving time and money.

A - be ACCOUNTABLE for your actions and those of your team.

C - be COMMITTED to being successful, and have open COMMUNICATIONS. Commitment and Communicating is everyone's responsibility.

T - be TEAMWORK oriented, with everyone connected with the tasks, including subcontractors, whether in the office or in the field. If the project finishes on or ahead of schedule, with little or no problems, no cost overruns, a level of TRUST is generated, and subcontractors will want to work with your company on future projects.

I - IDENTIFY problems early, and thereby possible solutions that can be generated early, saving time and money. Forestalling possible solutions only magnifies the issue, costing time and money.

V - VALIDATE everything and see that the SCAFFOLD is in place, i.e.:

Schedule/ Safety
Cost
Accountability
Foundation
Fabrication
Organization
Logistics
Determination

E - EXCELLING and EXCEEDING clients expectations, could have long term benefits for the company or agency you work for, in that you could have generated a repeat client, without advertising.

By Exceeding clients Expectations, several things can happen:

1) Clients talk to their friends and investors about how successful the project was, and how the project was finished on time, on or under budget, with few problems.

2) The subcontractors/suppliers that are hired, will see that they are part of the Team, and treated fairly, and will want to bid to your company with less "contingency" in their numbers.

3) The Architects and Engineers will talk with their "clients" about your company and how well your company performed, and who should bid on their projects.

4) The personnel of your company will take pride in what they as a Team accomplished

and will want to continue within the same framework and philosophy.

There is one other point that should be considered when using the word PROACTIVE, and that is it should not be used to criticize others, particularly young people. Young people want to learn and participate in the workings of the company that hired them. They may not know all the answers, but sitting in on some of the meetings with people that have experience, and to see how a team effort can communicate with each other and help solve potential problems ahead of time, without being criticized, goes a long way to making them a future asset.

Managers sometimes feel threatened by people under their control, and criticize them in front of others. By doing this, the whole idea of being part of team in a meeting and trying to contribute to help solve issues goes by the wayside. No one wants to bring up a "potential problem", as they may be criticized for being the one responsible for creating it in the first place, or not finding a solution sooner.

It does not matter what kind of business you are involved with, there will always be problems. Finding solutions takes a team effort, and being PROACTIVE will help generate positive results, before the problems occur, making the business endeavor very successful, and generally leads to:

PROFIT ABILITY

There is one "business institution" made up of five hundred thirty six people that control the largest budget in the world, where the words PROACTIVE and REACTIVE mean basically the same thing, and in either case could have negative results. That institution is:

The UNITED STATES GOVERNMENT

and includes the: PRESIDENT, SENATE,
& HOUSE OF
REPRESENTATIVES

To run for President of the USA could cost several hundreds of millions of dollars, and to run for Congress, whether it be as a Senator or Representative, could cost tens of millions of dollars. Where does this money come from? Investors of course!

We know, that in general, people "invest" their money to get a "return" on their investment, whether it is in the stock market, property, a business, or whatever, but it is something you can see and keep track of, and if it starts to show negative results you can sell it and/or invest in something else. In economic terms Supply and Demand. If there is a demand for a product, and you can supply it, you can make a profit.

Politicians run for office, knowing full well that they are probably going to be criticized by the opposing party, that the "position" may be only part time, but if they can get policies passed that are in "demand" from their investors, then both the politician and investor can garner very high "profits", and whether the politician is either PROACTIVE or REACTIVE, does not make a difference.

If politicians, regardless of party affiliation, were to use these words, they could have a number of definitions and meanings, and to a large extent it doesn't matter what the issue is, and whether or not the issue will raise taxes, create or delete jobs.

How politicians perform depends on which side of an issue their "their investors are on", and how well the "advertising" and all of the "press releases" are generated and handled.

PROACTIVE for politicians could
have multiple meanings.

1. Politicians React Only After Collecting on Their Investors Validation of Earmarks

2. Profitable Returns Originate After Collaborating w/Their Investors Very Effectively

3. Power grabbing Results in Overthrowing the American Constitution while Taxing

Individuals for Valuable Earmarks

REACTIVE for politicians could mean the following:

1. React Expediently After Collecting on Their Investors Valuable Earmarks

2. Repealing Entitlements Aggravates Contributors without Taxing Individuals to Validate these Entitlements

3. Ratifying Earmark Accounts Causes Tax Increases for Validating these Earmarks

4. Regulate Everything Actively & Collect Taxes Incessantly, for Validating Everything

Listening to politicians today is as Harry G. Frankfurt, Professor Emeritus of Philosophy at

Princeton University, stated in his book; "ON BULLSHIT"; Copyright 2005, by Princeton University Press stated in his book as follows:

In his book he writes: "The realms of advertising and of public relations, and the nowadays closely related realm of politics, are replete with instances of bullshit so unmitigated that they can serve among the most indisputable and classic paradigms of the concept."

At the end of year 2010, the deficit of the United States reached Fourteen Trillion Dollars ($14,000,000,000,000), and it is going up every day. Why?

Our "national business" leaders, i.e. politicians continue spending on programs that have no positive results by trying to control the free enterprise system, raising taxes, and causing problems that go wildly beyond any decent business venture. There is no planning as to what these policies will do to the nation, what they will cost, and the individual taxpaying citizens, whether they be liberal, conservative, or independent will bear the burden.

In Thomas Cleary's book the Art of War, be writes that Sun Tzu says, "while war is never to be initiated by the military itself, but by command of the civilian government, however, an absentee civilian leadership that interferes ignorantly with field command takes away victory by deranging the military."

The United States is in an economic war, and it was not started by the private enterprise system of the United States, that has been the backbone of America's freedom of free enterprise system since 1776.

Our economic system is being "deranged", by the continuing policies of our government and the politicians that are dictating:

What companies can do and what "rules" they have to follow.

> Where they can do or not do it.
> Who should do it?
> When to do it?
> Why to do it.
> How to do it?

How and why is it that for every American product, there are six to eight products that are made in China, imported from China into the United States, and cost almost thirty percent less than an American made product?

We cannot tell what the product is made of, how it was made, what material was used, and we hardly impose any great "taxes" on their products, versus American made products that are highly taxed here in this country, as well as those that are shipped overseas.

We import oil from overseas, which costs the American consumer more money, when we have our own oil, but the restrictions that are imposed on American companies, from environmental groups and our government, which cannot be imposed on foreign countries, makes drilling here more expensive. Why? And is not some of this money being paid to these foreign countries being used to finance a "terrorist war" against the United States?

The result of these policies is that the "economic" war is being lost, because we cannot compete, even though we know what the problem is, but we are not planning or proposing any solutions, taxes on the American public are skyrocketing, hurting all Americans, except those politicians that are benefiting from their own definition of Proactive or Reactive.

So what should be the definition of PROACTIVE mean for politicians? Politicians are elected to protect two documents: The Declaration of Independence, and the Constitution of the United States of America. To do that, politicians must:

P - PLAN ahead as to how the laws, and bills, that they may want to enact, will impact these two documents, and what will be the cost impact on the American people, and the Free Trade System.

R - be RESPONSIBLE for their actions to the "citizens" of the United States and not to their "investors" and their entitlements and or earmarks.

O - ORGANIZE policies and programs that benefit our economy, rather than hurt it, so that these policies generate "profits" rather than "deficits", and be OPEN book about what these policies will cost, and lower tax rates rather than raising them.

A - be ANALYTICAL about everything, and see to it that the ACTIONS taken are in response to needs of this America, and it's people, it's true "investors".

C - be COMMITTED to the Constitution, and consider how their actions will affect the people that believe in this document.

T - over TAXING accomplishes only negative results on free enterprise and the people, and while politicians are elected to manage our country, they have to provide the TEAM i.e.

the "American people" with policies that make us winners, and not losers.

I - IDENTIFY the problems of policies and the cost impact on the American people.

V - VALIDATE everything that their actions will have on the "business" they were "hired" to work for, so as not to have losses and deficits for the people they represent.

E - ENTITLEMENTS and EARMARKS, which only help and prosper the few, by taxing the many was not what our elected officials were "hired" to do. The elimination of this kind of business must be a priority, if financial success for the USA is to be achieved.

If politicians conducted and performed their duties they were elected for, which in reality is to conduct the operations of the government as a "business enterprise", without over spending, over taxing, over regulating all of the people, and private business, i.e., their "clients", we could have a thriving economy as we have had in the past. If they exceeded and excelled their "clients" expectations, they would be seen as being PROACTIVE in the real world, and maybe their "jobs" would not be so part time.

If they continue to conduct business as usual in the herein outlined political meaning of PROACTIVE or REACTIVE, this "business" will continue to fail, as it is currently doing, and this country of the United States and its citizens will suffer the consequences. A successful business cannot last long with a deficit that grows every day, for we all know what that could lead to:

BANKRUPTCY

and then we all could be working for China, trying to pay off "our" debt to them, that our politicians created, and then the whole country could be in foreclosure.

Proof of the idea of BANKRUPTCY in the U.S.A. being caused by politicians, in particular, the President, who was elected in 2008, whom few people knew anything about, can be found in the deficit of the USA. At the end of 2008 the deficit was about 9 Trillion Dollars. In four years, this newly elected President, who had not presented a budget in these 3 years, has increased the deficit to 15 Trillion Dollars, due to extravagant spending on programs and companies that have gone bankrupt in a short period of time, and the unemployment rate reached the highest it has been in decades.

The President's solution to the problem is to increase taxes on the rich and American business, hire more people to work for the government, so that the government can "Dictate" and "Regulate" everything "WE THE PEOPLE" can do, by dictating: WHO can do it, WHAT they can do, WHERE they can do it, WHEN they can do it, WHY they have to do it, and HOW they have to do it, no matter what it cost, as there was no budget to begin with.

This is not Free Enterprise or "CAPITALISM", but it is "SOCIALISM", which according to a college classmate, is what this President also studied in college besides law, and based on his performance over his first 4 years, he must have gotten an A+ for his final grade in Socialism, however his grade as the leader of the United States of America is F-.

The only thing left for this President to do, after putting an end to CAPITALISM and FREE ENTERPRISE, is to put an end to FREE SPEECH, which is what the liberal press is trying to do thanks to “investors” like George Soros.

GOD HELP US! OOP’s - We may not be able to say this as the current administration, which was re-elected in 2012, is silently endorsing Socialism.

About the Author

Mr. Panachyda is a graduate of Newark College of Engineering, with a Bachelor of Science in Mechanical Engineering.

He was working for an engineering/design firm for about four years, when he was drafted in the army in 1970. He did his basic training at Fort Lewis in the state of Washington and was sent to Picatinney Arsenal in Dover, New Jersey. He received a patent for an idea he had and was honorably discharged in 1972, with the rank of SPS.

He went back to engineering and construction in New York City and, after five years, was asked by the president of the company if he would consider going to Brazil to represent the company as part of a joint venture with a Brazilian developer in Sao Paulo, Brazil.

After two years, Mr. Panachyda found out that the joint venture partner was using joint venture funds for his private ventures. The joint venture was dissolved, and Mr. Panachyda was asked if he would stay on as general manager for the American company, which he did for ten years until the company was bought by a German company, who also had an office in Sao Paulo.

It was during these ten years that Mr. Panachyda began to use the words "proactive vs reactive" with his staff, both in the field and main office to see that problems would not arise, so as not to increase costs or add time to the schedules, which could impact the clients' budget.

www.ingramcontent.com/pod-product-compliance
Ingram Content Group UK Ltd.
Pitfield, Milton Keynes, MK11 3LW, UK
UKHW021051270726
13967UKWH00012B/205

9 781504 910934